A Guide to Copywriting Which Will Grow your Business.

By M. Sobaan Saeed

Contents

What is Copywriting & Why Is It So Important?

Simply put, copywriting is the writing you use in your written promotional
materials. This can include your advertising, website, brochure, catalogs,
business cards, sales letter and more.

Copywriting is what you use to get your customers and potential customers to
take a particular action. For example:

- Call you for more information
- Place an order
- Sign up for your mailing list
- Get them to refer a friend to your business

Many business owners make the mistake of thinking they can just throw their

copywriting together. I congratulate you for taking the time to read this guide
because the information in it will put you ahead of many other small business
owners who make this mistake.

1 The Basics of Copywriting:

In this chapter, I'll go over some terminology that will help you in understanding

the principles of copywriting. Read each one in detail as I've not only included the

definition of each word, but I've also added:

• Examples and further detail for deeper understanding of these important concepts.

• Exercises to apply these concepts.

This information will serve as your foundation of knowledge in all the

copywriting you do for your business.

You're not there to answer people's inquiries or persuade them of the superiority of your goods while they browse your website or read your brochure. That must be done for you by your words. To put it another way, you require good copywriting.

1.1   Identify Target Market

The demographic to which you are marketing your product is known as your target market. To make your copywriting the most effective, you must be very particular when defining your target market. Simply stating "women, moms, or pet owners" is insufficient because it is still ambiguous.

There are several factors to consider when determining your target market. Below is a brief list that merely scratches the surface. There are so many distinct elements that might make up your particular target market for each target market:

- Age
- Income
- Interests
- If it's a woman, her marital status may come into play

- If it's a mom, you might want to have an idea about the age of her children; if she works outside the home, etc.
- If it's a pet owner, what kind of pet she has, what breed, etc.

The following are significant human motivators that psychologists have found. They will aid you in comprehending the driving forces behind your readers' behaviour:

- Fear
- Exclusivity
- Guilt
- Greed
- Need for approval
- Convenience
- Pleasure

However, you may use this knowledge to truly understand what drives your target market. Some people would view it as dishonest to play too much on the emotions of their potential customer. It will be simpler to sell to your target market if you have a better understanding of them.

You will comprehend their perspective, the issues they are experiencing, and how eager they are for a solution.

Think about your Ideal Customer:

What does she long for and want? What issues does she want to get resolved? Try doing a survey of your current clients if you don't already know that. Ask them a few questions about themselves, the product they purchased, what they like and dislike about it. Offer them anything in exchange—a voucher, a cost-free item, etc.—just to obtain their input. You will find this knowledge to be useful.

Now Think about your Product:

What is the single most important reason your target audience would want to buy it? You must be able to relate to your target market, recognize their concerns, and demonstrate how your product addresses those issues. It's difficult to get people passionate about anything if you think too broadly about your target market and your content loses its fire.

You might make some sales, for instance, if you merely discuss the embarrassment of acne while selling acne treatment. However, your copywriting will be far more effective if you know that your target market for a certain ad campaign includes teens who talk about being mocked at school, worry that they won't find a date, and have a case study of a teenager who overcame those issues.

Each product you offer may have a somewhat or even significantly different market if you sell related products that are sold in combination (for instance, skin cream and eye makeup). It's conceivable that a lady in her 30 s who wants to minimize wrinkles will be drawn to the skin cream if it reduces wrinkles and the eye makeup has a glittering blue color. A younger, trendier audience is more likely to enjoy the glittering blue eye shadow. There are, of course, exceptions, and if you sell cosmetics, you have the chance to get to know your market the best. You can still recognize variations in your target market, even within your own product line, and your text should reflect these.

Additionally, it's likely that you have more than one highly niche market for a specific product. If so, you can develop various promotional materials to speak to those audiences. For instance, if you sell that wrinkle cream and learn that males are also interested in it in addition to certain types of women, you may develop promotional materials to address the issues and preferences of each group. So you can give people the proper marketing materials for your various advertising campaigns and promotions.

Exercise:

Start outlining all the traits that your typical consumer possesses. Write at least 15-20 distinct qualities using the data from consumer surveys that was mentioned before in this part. You can use this list to your advantage as you navigate this eBook.

1.2   Tell Benefits

The advantages your customer experiences because of using your product are your benefits. Benefits typically sell your items better than features do, as was indicated in the definition of features. Although effective writing incorporates both, the

Most of the product text should emphasize the advantages.

Example: You sell a ballpoint pen

The features are black ink, a felt tip, and it comes with a lid.
The benefits are that it reduces hand cramping and eliminates smudges.

Observe how the pen sounds like any other pen when we discuss its attributes but sounds more fascinating when we discuss its advantages.

These are advantages that support the sale of your goods. People desire to purchase your goods to solve an issue they have. Expose to them the advantages of your product.

What If Your Clients are Interested in Features?

When you sell a product, clients may frequently compare its attributes.

Internet service for companies could be one illustration of this. Companies who

require Internet access desire to learn about the costs, the speed, etc. An industry with intense feature competition and attention is internet service. By highlighting some of their service's advantages, you can still distinguish yourself from the competition.

Inform potential customers about your high uptime rate and the fact that they won't have to worry about losing sales if their websites go down more frequently than with other service providers. In this illustration, the advantage is not losing sales while the feature is uptime, which makes it easier for potential consumers to understand why they would use your service. Thoughts like "Oh sure, if it's not up, I'm going to lose a transaction" are what your target market has when they consider up-time to be more than just a metric Internet service providers tout. That is the sort of stuff you want to discuss with them.

Another illustration would be to state that you answer support tickets or phone calls within an hour. Describe yourself as the "stress-free Internet service provider that assures your business can run as it should be 24 hours a day, seven days a week." Once more, having a response within an hour is a feature, but the advantage is reduced stress and not losing out on crucial business time.

Exercise:

List a benefit for each feature on the list of features you just made in the preceding example. In addition to assisting, you in comprehending the advantages of your product, this list will enable you to complete a significant component of the product's text. You can include that information on your website or brochure in a bullet point fashion.

1.3   Bullets Points

Bullets are one of the greatest things you'll come to love about copywriting. They
are relatively easy to write and they can also sell your product exceptionally well.
The following are examples of bullet points:

• What exactly a transcriptionist does and why her services are in such
demand.

• Perks of having your own transcriptionist business: Learn about the low
start-up costs, how to set your own hours and work with the flexibility
this business provides.

As we demonstrated in the previous two tasks, bullets might be about the features of your items or their advantages, and frequently they will mention both.

It's simple to convey a lot of information about your product using bullet points. Efficiently and successfully to your potential customer. They could have trouble reading it if you formatted it completely in paragraph style.

Additionally, bullet points might "tease" readers into being more interested in your offering. When you're promoting a course, book, or other instructional product, this is especially beneficial. A smart bullet point teases the reader about what is contained and encourages them to buy without revealing the information you are offering. Of course, you don't want to offer your goods for free!

Example:

Bad bullet point:

- Passionately kiss your husband each morning and he's sure to stay faithful.

Good bullet point:

- Do this one thing each morning and your
  husband's eyes will never stray
  to another woman.

The first bullet point gives away what's in your
information product. The other
one tells the BENEFIT of what's included (the faithful
husband), but doesn't tell
you how to do it

1.4 Headlines

Your headline should appear at the very top of every piece of text you write, including ads, web pages, sales letters, and so on. To ensure that your headline attracts attention, capitalize each word and make it beautiful and big and bold.

Every effective piece of writing has a catchy title. People are busy; therefore, you only have a brief window of opportunity to capture their interest. If you don't grab their attention, they won't read the fine print on your page. You can do this with the aid of a direct, benefit-focused headline.

A headline that merely states, "We Sell X Widgets," is insufficient to pique a reader's interest. Most likely many of individuals market X Widgets. What makes them want to know more about yours?

Here are a few headline ideas if you're having difficulties coming up with one. You can use these highly popular strategies—which have been demonstrated to work—for your copy or try something altogether different. These are merely some ideas to get your brain working:

- **"Who Else Wants to"**

This is an easy way to start; relate to your audience.

Example: "Who Else Wants to Save Up to 50% on Their Phone Bill? Try Our Rates Calculator to Find the Best Deals on Long Distance. "

- **"How_____Made me_____and It Can Help You Too"**

Example: "How X-Brand Weight-Loss Shake Made Me Lose 37 Pounds in 7 Weeks".

- **Are You_____?"**

Example: "Are You Tired of Unsightly Bags under Your Eyes? Apply Just a Dab of X Cream

Once a Day for 6 Days and Watch the Puffiness Disappear.

- **"The Secrets to___"**

Everybody loves secrets...tell them about yours.

Example: "The Secrets to Rekindling the Romance with Your Husband"

- **"Give Me___and I'll_____"**

Example: "Give me 15 Days and I'll turn Your Ever-Reluctant Child into an Avid Reader".

Tell them what they have to put in to it and what benefit they will get out of it.

Exercise:

Visit a couple websites or peruse the ads in a magazine or newspaper. Check out what catches your eye. Can you use those concepts in your headline?

1.5   Sub-Headlines

In your sales copy, sub-headlines are supplementary headlines. Sub-headlines typically aren't as large as the other headlines in your material, but they will be bold and use capital letters to draw attention.

Your material will be easier to read if you use subheadings to break it up. Additionally, it aids in capturing the interest of readers who are skimming rather than reading your sales copy.

Every few paragraphs, use sub-headlines to highlight significant portions of your material. Use benefits and be explicit in your sub-headlines.

Example:

If you've prepared marketing content for your free weekly email newsletter, you should use sub-headlines to bring readers' attention to key passages.

You might have a sub-headline that says: When you are about to include some bullet points regarding what is contained in your newsletter.

Here's What's Included in Your Free Subscription to ____

Then, just before you introduce your subscription form, you can have a sub-headline that says:

Claim Your Free Subscription by Completing the Simple Form Below

Those are simply examples and copy that is more than a couple of paragraphs can be broken up in that manner.

Exercise:

If you've already written some longer material or are about to start writing some, look for opportunities to add sub-headlines. You can see how it catches the eye, makes material easier to find for skimmers, and helps readers understand instructions visually.

1.6   Call to Action

After reading your promotional material, your call-to-action is what you want your reader to do. It might be as easy as making a phone call to you for further details, joining your mailing list, or purchasing your goods. Unless you do

People are less inclined to carry out your instructions if you tell them. Even while your text suggests customers purchase your goods, if you don't explicitly ask for the sale, you won't make it as frequently.

There should be a call to action in every piece of sales writing. It doesn't matter if it's a page on your website, a card you hand out, or another piece of copywriting.

Examples: Here are some examples of a call-to-action:

- Click a link to place an order
- Call a 1-800 number to place an order
- Call a number to hear a recorded message
- Fill in a form to enter a sweepstakes

Tip: A call to action is simple to add to the back of your business card. Invite your contacts to visit your website to download a sample, join up for your free newsletter, or perform any other action you desire.

Exercise:

Examine each page of the marketing materials you've created. Make sure there is a call to action. Fix it if it doesn't. If your company is just getting off the ground, keep this in mind while you design each page of your website, business cards, etc.

1.7   Offer/Pricing

An offer is simply what you are selling/giving to your readers.

Example:

A personalized baby blanket with embroidery is what you're selling. For $35, you can give your customer a 3' by 3' blanket with an embroidered message up to 25 letters in the color and pattern of their choice. An additional fee applies to additional designs.

Another Example:

It's not necessary to trade money to accept an offer. You may provide a free weekly email subscription with gardening advice in exchange for a first name and email address.

Your call to action and your offer is related, but they are not the same thing. Your offer is what you will provide in exchange for the money or other item(s) you are requesting. The particular instructions you provide for your potential customer to accept your offer are known as the call-to-action.

Exercise:

Spend some time outlining every aspect of your own offer in writing. Be as explicit as possible, as I did in the instances above.

2 Tips for Writing Great Copy

These are some more suggestions to assist you in creating excellent copy now that you are aware of some of the key language used in copywriting and how to make the most of those components.

2.1   Speak to Your Audience

It's simple to make the error of talking about oneself excessively in your **sales** copy given that It's meant to sell your own items. The issue is that your prospective client doesn't care about you. They are concerned about themselves, seeking answers to their issues as well as information about what you can do to help. Prioritize your customer's needs first.

Many sales materials place too much emphasis on the company performing the selling:

"We believe in customer satisfaction..."

It's simple enough to change wording around to focus more on "you" and how you can help your potential customer. Turn it around and write things like this instead:

"Your satisfaction is guaranteed..."

Exercise:

Change many of the "we" to "you' in your material, then edit it to reflect the shift in emphasis. When you're finished, you'll be able to connect with your readers far more. The emphasis is on your future client, even if you'll typically be stating essentially the same thing (for instance, "We believe in customer satisfaction" is like "Your contentment is assured").

2.2 Avoid Excessive Adjectives

Can you see what's wrong with the following copywriting example?

"The biggest and best e-book that will make you the happiest person on your block."

The Problem: That line above is meaningless, aside from the fact that it makes some extravagant claims. The size of an eBook isn't really important, and this statement doesn't exactly explain why it's the greatest. Additionally, the term "happiest" is somewhat meaningless. We all want to be happy, but if we're not right now, there are issues that need to be resolved. Telling someone they will be happy doesn't really solve their problems. They are curious about how you plan to make them happy and solve their individual issues.

The fundamental issue with the previous statement is the abundance of adjectives that give no specifics. Adjectives describe nouns but don't give readers any information. Make sure you answer these questions in your copy:

- How are you the best?
- What makes you great?
- How do you care for your customer

What people want to know is that. If you use too many adjectives, the message is lost, and it comes off as overly hyped. This does not preclude you from using adjectives in your writing. Naturally, you'll still utilize them, but your copy should be strong enough to stand on its own without them.

Exercise:
Remove all the adjectives from a few paragraphs on your website or the full page to determine if your copy can stand on its own.
Is it still interesting to you? Is it promoting your goods?

2.3   Be on Point

When I wrote about headlines, I made a quick mention of this. Let's explore this further and fully get how being might assist you in selling more of your offering.

Say WHY you are the greatest rather than simply asserting that you ARE the best. rather than saying

You're quick; specify how and in what precise manner. Tell them the average amount of time it takes you to complete a project, for example, if you are a printing company and you provide quick printing. You shouldn't use that perspective if you won't state how quickly you can finish a task because it suggests that you're probably not that quick.

When we talk about copy, we mean providing readers with as much specific information as possible so they can decide whether to purchase a product, subscribe to a newsletter, or respond to another call to action.

Have you ever visited a website and considered purchasing a product but weren't absolutely certain it offered the features or benefits you required? It frequently takes place. Many product vendors believe that all they need to do is add a picture and a few words to generate sales. Sadly, things don't work that way.

There is no such thing as providing too much information about your goods. There is no such thing as giving consumers too much information if you are providing them with the knowledge they need to make a purchasing decision. Yes, being overly wordy can make your reader drowsy. You want to satisfy all of their inquiries so they will buy.

Quantifying things is another effective strategy for being precise. Tell them there are 37 strategies to lower your cholesterol if you have an eBook with that information. Don't imply that there are "many ways" or that this booklet is filled with suggestions to lower your cholesterol. Additionally, a precise number like 37 tends to elicit a more positive response than a round number like 30. It's not entirely obvious why this happens, but it's probably because round numbers can come off as made up or speculative, whereas when you say 37, it conjures up a certain image in their minds.

Exercise:

Take a look at the writing you've done for your company. Can you please be more specific? What is measurable?

2.4   Don't Worry about Grammar

There will be folks who advise you to use good grammar to project a professional image as you go about running your business. Some of the people who visit your website might even take the time to email you to express their outrage at the spelling and grammar errors. Don't worry yourself too much about this. Read on to learn why grammar isn't as important as it's made up to be. Correct the spelling, and if the grammar is outrageous, change it.

Your sales copy's or articles' most crucial components should sound natural and suitably relate to your target audience. Write how you would speak.

Naturally, you might need to use a more professional tone and pay closer attention to grammar standards if your audience is PHD students who are studying literature.

You might write and speak more casually if your target audience includes people interested in fashion trends or race cars.

Since most markets will be more relaxed, you should use your text to project a warm and genuine picture. It's acceptable to occasionally begin sentences with "and" and "but" because that's how we communicate and how you write.

Speaking affects how you connect with your audience. Again, since that's how we communicate, it's acceptable to conclude a sentence with a preposition.

Exercise:

Analyze your writing to see whether it is professional or casual. Can you think of any improvements you could make to make it sound friendlier and more inviting to the reader? You risk completely losing your audience if you are overly formal. Being natural is preferable to sounding uninformed. Although the majority of your grammar will be correct, you don't necessarily need to care about some rules for readability.

2.5   Keep it Simple

To make your writing easier to read, use brief sentences. To prevent eye fatigue, break up long paragraphs. Once more, it's acceptable to defy the norms of grammar, especially when it comes to paragraph structuring because reading lengthy paragraphs might be tiresome. Online and other places where people are reading on screens, this is especially true. Don't exhaust your prospective buyer before they have a chance to learn about your offering.

As we just said, you can use bullet points, and they may contain phrases that aren't fully formed. Fortunately, that is permissible according to grammatical standards! Making it simple to read is the key.

Make sure the wording is simple and acceptable for your target audience. The general people has a very poor average reading ability. Always define a word, even if you think a more sophisticated term would be more appropriate, in case your readers are unaware of its meaning.

2.6   Create Sense of Urgency – Get them to Buy Now

After reading about your product, consumers can be enthusiastic about it, but they might also decide to wait to buy. The issue is that most of the time when people resolve to buy later, they never do. They'll misplace your brochure, toss your advertisement out of the newspaper, or forget the URL of your website.

You need to convey a sense of urgency to avoid this. Make them feel as though they must purchase right away, in other words. Here are some strategies for encouraging immediate purchase:

- Offer a time-limited discount
- Limit the distribution of your product
- Offer them extra bonuses or goodies with your product, but only for a
limited time.
- Show them how serious their particular problem is and why they should
find a solution now

The more you can convince them to buy right now, the more probable it is that you'll close the deal.

Exercise:

Check all your marketing materials to see if you can add a feeling of urgency. You can always add a small sense of urgency, whether it's to motivate them to find a solution to their problem right away or to give a limited-time discount.

2.7   Close the Deal

Never neglect to make the selling request. Tell them
specifically what you want them to do whether you
want them to phone you for further information, fill
out a form, or join a mailing list. The call-to-action
was defined in the section before, but it merits
repeating.

Your call-to-action can include:

- A summary of your offer.
- Your price and why the price provides good value.
- Specific instruction on how to complete the call to
action.

I've given you the basics of what it takes to develop
good sales copy in the previous two chapters. You
have several possibilities to return and compete if
your firm is already established. The majority of small
firms rely more on one-on-one selling and follow-up
because they don't fully understand copywriting.

While you will probably still engage in some person-to-person marketing, as a busy mother with excellent authoring abilities, you can cut out a lot of the tedious labor! Enhance your sales communications. You are already ahead of most of your small business competitors if you are just getting started.

3 Conclusion

When you aren't present to close the sale, copywriting can help. You are not physically present to personally welcome website visitors. How will someone remember you when they glance at your business card a few weeks after first meeting you? If you distribute brochures, make sure they are compelling enough to compel customers to make a purchase from you.

All your marketing communications should be created using the copywriting fundamentals as a guide.

The language you use on your website, business card, or brochure says a lot about you and your company. Verify the message you're conveying.

Your copywriting will be successful with a little planning, practice, and persistence!